# MEET ALL THESE FRIENDS IN BUZZ BOOKS:

Thomas the Tank Engine
The Animals of Farthing Wood
Biker Mice From Mars
James Bond Junior
Joshua Jones
Fireman Sam
Rupert
Babar

First published in Great Britain 1993 by Buzz Books,
an imprint of Reed Children's Books
Michelin House, 81 Fulham Road, London SW3 6RB
and Auckland, Melbourne, Singapore and Toronto
Reprinted 1993 (twice)

The Animals of Farthing Wood © copyright 1979 Colin Dann
Storylines © copyright EBU 1992
Text © copyright 1993 William Heinemann Ltd
Illustrations © copyright 1993 William Heinemann Ltd
Based on the novels by Colin Dann and the animation series
produced by Telemagination and La Fabrique for the BBC
and the European Broadcasting Union.

All rights reserved.

ISBN 1 85591 2805

Printed and bound in Italy by Olivotto

# Fire!

Story by Colin Dann
Text by Mary Risk
Illustrations by The County Studio

The animals of Farthing Wood had been travelling all night. Now at last they slept.

Badger dreamed of his old set. Tomorrow, giant digger machines would destroy it.

Owl dreamed of her favourite perch. The big oak tree had been sawn down already to make room for new houses.

Fox slept lightly. As leader of the animals, he had to be watchful, day and night.

"Follow me, mateys," croaked Toad in his sleep. "I'm the only one who knows the way to the nature reserve. It's safe there."

And what about Mole? He was dreaming of fat, juicy worms, as usual.

Suddenly, there was a huge explosion.

"A-an earthquake!" cried Mother Rabbit.

"Don't panic!" squealed Father Rabbit. "Oh, my poor nerves!"

"It seems the shooting season's started early," said Fox. "How very unsporting."

Kestrel flew off to see what was happening.

"Kee! Kee!" she called, coming in to land.
"There are soldiers! This is army land."

"It's time to travel on," said Fox.

"But where's Mole?" said Badger.

A little snout pushed up through the
earth, and the rest of Mole followed it.

"Sorry," he said, gulping down a worm.
"Just finishing my breakfast."

9

Kestrel led them down to the marsh.

"Come on, Baby," said Mother Newt
wearily. "We're going for a swim."

"Water!" squeaked Baby Newt. "Water!"

They flopped into the cool marsh with a
sigh of relief. Toad followed right behind.
Fox looked at them anxiously.

"You're tired out already," he said.

"Don't worry about me," croaked Toad
bravely. "I like long walks. But the newts
can't go on. Why don't they stay here?"

"Yes!" said the newts. "We'll stay here."

"All right," said Fox. "Good luck, newts."

"Hooray!" squeaked Baby Newt. "We're
going to live in the marsh!" He splashed the
water with his tail.

Fox rounded up the other animals.

"We must get round the marsh before
nightfall," he said. "It's time to go."

"Must we?" said Mole. "The worms here
are the biggest, nicest, juiciest..."

"One day, Mole," said Owl severely,
"you'll be so fat you'll get stuck in one of
your own tunnels."

12

They set off. Adder was behind the mice.

"I sssimply adore a fat moussse," she teased.

The mice scattered in terror.

"Adder!" barked Fox. "Stop that!"

No one saw the car that passed along the road behind them, or the careless human tossing a cigarette end into the dry grass.

Weasel was the first to smell the smoke.

"Fire!" she squealed. "And I'm not joking this time! Honest!"

The rabbits had been fooled before.

"You're teasing, as usual," they said.

"Since we've stopped anyway..." muttered Mole, sliding off Badger's back. A minute later, he was digging for worms.

"Where's Toad?" asked Fox. "We mustn't
lose our guide. Where..."

Suddenly, Kestrel swooped down. "Fire!
Fire!" she mewed. "Danger! Run!"

The rabbits quivered in terror.

"Don't panic! Don't panic!" shrieked
Mother Rabbit, bolting the wrong way.

"Come back!" shouted Badger gruffly.
"We must stick together!"

Fox could see the fire now. He could feel
the heat of the flames, and hear their
terrifying crackle. Clouds of billowing smoke
made him cough and splutter. His instinct
told him to run, but he stood his ground.

"I must save the others," he thought.
"And I must find Toad! He's our guide!"

"Kestrel!" he called. "Lead everyone to the other side of the marsh! The big ones must go slowly, and wait for the smallest."

"We can't go yet," said Badger anxiously. "We've lost Mole! And Adder!"

Adder slithered out of the smoke. "How sssweet of you to wait," she said.

"Oh Moley, where are you?" said Badger.

"Come now!" called Kestrel. "Follow me!
Kee! Kee!"

Fox was shaking with fear, but he ran
back towards the fire.

"Where are you going, Fox?" said Kestrel.

"I must find Toad!" replied Fox.

The smoke was choking him. The flames
were blinding him. But he ran on and on.

"Toad!" he called. "Where are you?"

Toad croaked feebly. He was crouching near the ground, waiting to die.

"I'm coming, Toad!" coughed Fox.

Toad looked up. "You came back for me," he gasped. "Thanks, matey."

Fox picked Toad up gently in his mouth, and ran out of the fire to safety.

While the fire raged overhead, Mole was busy digging underground. He heard Badger's voice calling to him, but just then a juicy worm caught his eye.

"A few more minutes won't hurt," he said greedily, and started gobbling up the worm. Finally, he dug his way up to the surface.

Mole made a little mound of earth as he
dug himself out of the ground. When he
popped to the surface, he found the fire
brigade dousing the flames with their long
hoses. The ground was charred and soaked.

A fireman saw him. "Poor little chap," he
said, and he picked Mole up and put him in
his pocket.

The fire was quickly spreading to the other
side of the marsh where the animals
bunched together anxiously.

Kestrel hovered, looking for a way out.
"Fox," she called. "There's an island, with a
causeway running out to it. You can cross
there. The water's shallow. But be quick!
The fire is getting closer!"

It was easy for the big animals to cross the causeway, but the little ones stood on the bank, chattering with fear.

"We can't cross on our own! We'll drown!" they squeaked.

"Climb aboard, then," said Badger.

The smaller animals climbed onto Badger and Fox and held on tightly as they crossed to the safety of the island.

Mole peeped out of the fireman's pocket.
The jacket was slung over the door of the
fire engine. Quickly, Mole scrambled out
of the pocket.

"Look, there's Mole!" called Kestrel.

"Moley will never find us here," said Fox.
"Owl, if you and Kestrel distract the
firefighters, I'll go and fetch him."

"Where are Badger and the others?" Mole
wondered as he climbed to the ground.

Just then, there was a "Whoo-hoo!" from
Owl, and a "Kee! Kee!" from Kestrel, and
the two birds soared into the air. They
dived and turned above the firefighters'
heads in a dazzling flying display.

The firefighters watched in amazement.

Fox saw his chance. He darted across the causeway and ran up to Mole, who was peering blindly round with his short-sighted eyes, not knowing which way to run.

"Quick! Climb up my tail!" said Fox.

"Wh-what? Wh-where?" said Mole. Then he saw Fox's brush, and jumped onto it.

One of the firefighters saw them.

"Cor! Look at that fox!" he said, and all the firefighters turned round.

"And there are more animals on that island!" said another. "Rabbits, hedgehogs, squirrels and a badger, all together. Poor little creatures. Let's leave them in peace."

The animals watched the firefighters go.

"Oh, thank you, Fox! Thank you!" sobbed Mole. "I've been so silly! I promise I'll never be greedy again. I thought I'd lost you forever, and I missed you so much, especially you, Badger."

Badger picked up his little friend. "And I missed you, Moley," he said.

A drop of rain fell on Toad's head.

"Ah-ha! Rain!" he chuckled happily.

"Not everyone likes rain," the rabbits sniffed. "We need to be warm and dry."

"Follow me, everyone," said Fox. "Let's go and look for shelter so we can have a rest."

"Good thinking, Fox!" said Badger, and all of the other animals agreed.